···TECH·TITANS···

THE GENIUS OF
GOOGLE

How Larry Page, Sergey Brin, and a
Search Engine Changed the World

Margaret J. Goldstein

Lerner Publications ◆ Minneapolis

Lerner Publications Company
An imprint of Lerner Publishing Group, Inc.
241 First Avenue North
Minneapolis, MN 55401 USA

For reading levels and more information, look up this title at www.lernerbooks.com.

Main body text set in Aptifer Sans LT Pro.
Typeface provided by Linotype AG.

Library of Congress Cataloging-in-Publication Data

Names: Goldstein, Margaret J., author.
Title: The genius of Google : how Larry Page, Sergey Brin, and a search engine changed the world / Margaret J. Goldstein.
Description: Minneapolis : Lerner Publications , [2022] | Series: Tech titans | Includes bibliographical references and index. | Audience: Ages 8–12 | Audience: Grades 4–6 | Summary: "Search engines allow us to find almost anything on the internet. But it wasn't always this easy. Find out more about the creation of Google, how it's expanded, and what's next for the innovative company"— Provided by publisher.
Identifiers: LCCN 2021022653 (print) | LCCN 2021022654 (ebook) | ISBN 9781728440842 (lib. bdg.) | ISBN 9781728449531 (pbk.) | ISBN 9781728445267 (eb pdf)
Subjects: LCSH: Google (Firm)—Juvenile literature. | Google—Juvenile literature. | Web search engines—Juvenile literature. | Page, Larry, 1973—-Juvenile literature. | Brin, Sergey, 1973—-Juvenile literature.
Classification: LCC TK5105.885.G66 G65 2022 (print) | LCC TK5105.885.G66 (ebook) | DDC 005.75/8—dc23

LC record available at https://lccn.loc.gov/2021022653
LC ebook record available at https://lccn.loc.gov/2021022654

Manufactured in the United States of America
1 – CG – 7/15/22

TABLE OF CONTENTS

The campus of Google's headquarters in Mountain View, California, is full of bikes for employees to ride from building to building.

The office in Palo Alto, California, looked like a playground for grown-ups. Workers lounged on yoga balls and decorated their desks with swirly lava lamps. They built with LEGO bricks. They brought their dogs, cats, and even pet lizards to the office. No question, this was a fun place to work. But when it came to their jobs, these workers were dead serious. They were the early employees of Google, and their accomplishments would change the world.

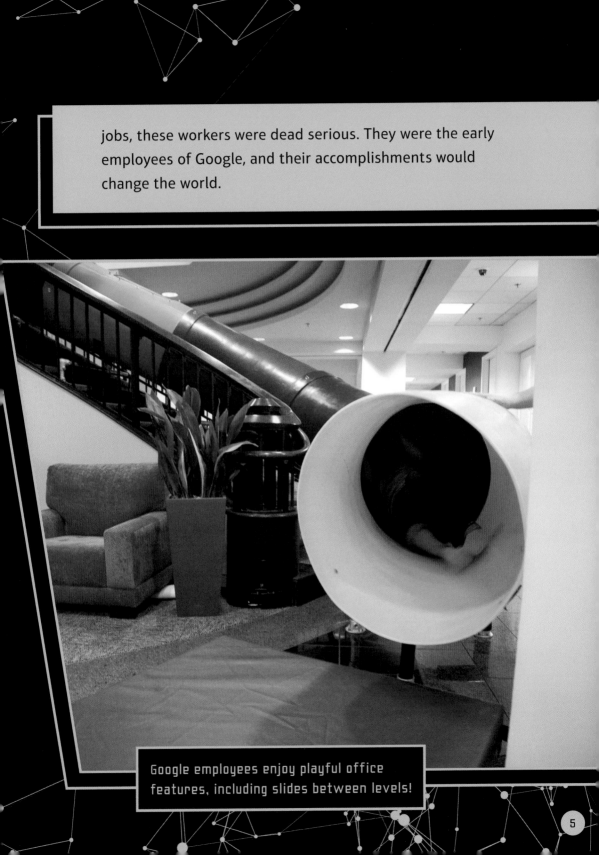

Stanford University is one of eight Ivy League schools in the United States. These schools are known for their academic excellence and social influence.

CHAPTER 1:
THE BEGINNING

Google began at Stanford University in California. There, in the summer of 1995, Sergey Brin met Larry Page. Brin was starting his second year of graduate school. Page would soon be a first-year graduate student. Both young men were studying computer science.

At this time, the World Wide Web was just a few years old. But it was growing quickly. By early 1996, the web had about one hundred thousand websites and ten million documents. Page was intrigued by all this data. He was particularly interested in the hyperlinks between web pages. He wanted to know which pages had the most backlinks, or links that connect from other sites. Incoming links were sort of like recommendations from other sites. So, pages with more backlinks were usually more informative and accurate than those with fewer backlinks.

For his final project, Page decided to map out the entire web and study the links. He used a crawler to search through the web, page by page and link by link. Meanwhile, Brin was interested in data mining. When he learned about Page's map of the web, he was intrigued. He loved the idea of studying the vast data on the web. He decided to join Page's project.

3rd Edition

Best of the Web Series

HOW TO SEARCH THE WEB

A Quick-Reference Guide to Finding Things
on the World Wide Web

Contents Summary

A 2000 guide to searching the web lists popular search engines at the time, including Infoseek, Lycos, and MetaCrawler.

SEARCH ME

Page and Brin did more than just gather data on web pages. They also ranked the pages according to their relevance. Their ratings were based on the number of backlinks coming into a page, as well as where those links connected to. For example, links from a university, government agency, or well-known newspaper got a higher rating than those from an unknown individual. Page and Brin realized that they had created more than just a map of the web. They had created a way to search for reliable, up-to-date, and accurate information. They had created a search engine.

Many other companies offered search engines at this time. But they didn't work very well. They often gave results from advertisers or untrustworthy sources. Meanwhile, Brin and Page's ranking system linked searchers with more relevant and reliable websites.

The two students chose a name for their search engine: Googol. This is the word for an incredibly large number— written as the number 1 followed by one hundred zeros. That word reflected the massive amount of data Brin and Page were studying. A fellow Stanford student checked to see if the domain name googol.com was already taken. But he typed in "google.com" by accident. Page and Brin liked the misspelled word. So on September 15, 1997, they registered the domain name Google.com.

Sergey Brin (*left*) and
Larry Page in 2008

OPEN FOR BUSINESS

Convinced they had built a superior search engine, Page and Brin took a chance. In 1998, instead of finishing their graduate degrees, they dropped out of Stanford and formed their own company. With a $100,000 investment from Andy Bechtolsheim, a cofounder of Sun Microsystems, Page and Brin were able to buy equipment, hire staff, and rent office space.

Andy Bechtolsheim calls his investment in Google "the best business decision I made in my life."

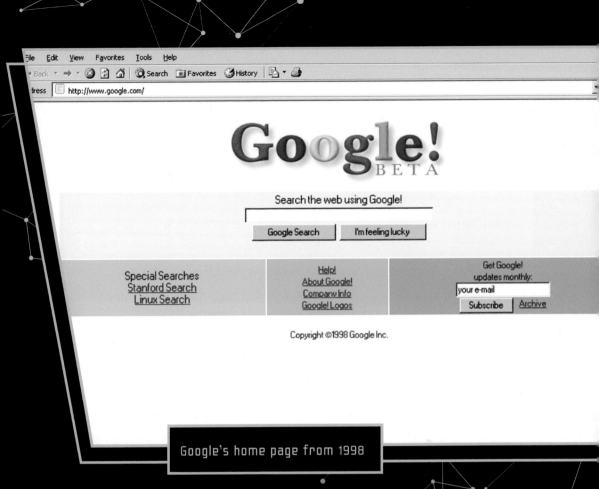

Google's home page from 1998

Meanwhile, the web grew to encompass millions of websites. People needed a reliable search engine to navigate the vast network of sites. Early users of Google spread the word about it. Articles in newspapers and magazines also led people to try Google. The company soon needed more staff and a bigger office space. People all over the world were now using the web, so Google built foreign-language versions of its search engine. By the summer of 2000, Google was processing about eighteen million searches a day.

Google was wildly popular, but it wasn't making money. At this time, most websites brought in cash by selling advertisements. Banner ads cluttered up web pages, urging site visitors to buy clothes, cars, food, and thousands of other products.

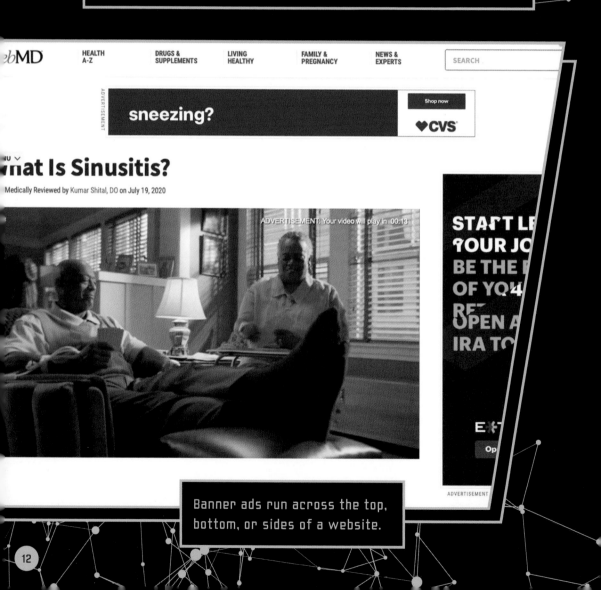

Banner ads run across the top, bottom, or sides of a website.

Google   cat toys

Q All   Shopping   Images   Videos   News   More   Tools

About 386,000,000 results (0.71 seconds)

Ads · Shop cat toys

One Fast Cat - Cat Exercise...	Chewy.com - PURRfect Leather...	Hammacher Schlemmer - The Award...	Chewy.com - Frisco Bird Teaser with...	Petco.com - Petstages Lil Avocato Ca...	Chewy.com - Petstages Tower of...	Amazon.com - Indoor Cat Interactive...	Chewy.com Goody Box Kitten Toys ...
$249.00	$7.19	$39.95	$2.88	$3.99	$11.99	$17.89	$24.99
One Fast Cat	Chewy.com	Hammacher ...	Chewy.com	Petco.com	Chewy.com	Amazon.com	Chewy.com
★★★★★ (1k+)	★★★★★ (1k+)	★★★★★ (369)	Free gift w/ ...	★★★★★ (110)	Special offer		★★★★★ (23)

Ad · https://www.chewy.com/cat/toys

Cat Toys at Chewy.com® - Up to 40% Off Cat Deals

Enter the Holi-YAY Shop for Up to 40% Off **Cat** Beds, Furniture, Apparel and More. **Cat Toys**, Keep Your Kitty Entertained, Shop Our Huge Selection of **Cat Toys**. 24/7 Customer Service. Helping 18,000+ Shelters. 35% Of

New Cat Checkl
Welcome Your Cat to t
Stock Up on New Pet E

> Companies bid to have their ads displayed with Google search results. Higher bids can help get an ad displayed higher up in the list of results.

Brin and Page didn't want banner ads on their site, but Google couldn't survive without income. So, it adopted a new approach to online advertising. When someone searched a keyword, such as "skateboarding," Google delivered its normal ranked search results: articles about skateboarders, skateboarding competitions, and skateboarding history from respected news outlets and organizations. But the searcher also got simple, text-based ads from skate shops and skateboard manufacturers. These were clearly labeled as ads and separated from the ranked results. If a searcher clicked on one of these ads, the advertiser paid Google. This pay-per-click model brought in cash for Google.

Google grew like crazy. In 2001, it had fewer than three hundred employees. By 2004, it had more than three thousand, with offices around the world. Every day, Google handled about two hundred million searches. The business name even became a verb, *google*, meaning to look something up online using Google. In 2006, reference book editors added the verb to their dictionaries.

Google's first international office opened in Tokyo, Japan, in 2001. In 2019, Google opened a second Tokyo office.

By the late 2000s, Google dominated the search engine market. Other popular search engines included Bing and Yahoo.

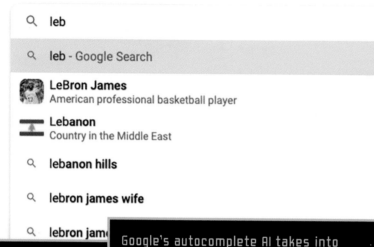

Google's autocomplete AI takes into account the user's language and location.

CHAPTER 2:
STANDOUT PRODUCTS

In 2021, Google was processing more than seven billion searches a day. Using algorithms and artificial intelligence (AI), Google continues its mission to deliver accurate, reliable, and up-to-date results. The search engine can even anticipate users' searches. For instance, if someone starts typing in "Leb . . .," Google might predict a search for basketball star LeBron James. If the user accidentally types "Leron James," Google will recognize the misspelling.

With Google, users can search translations in more than one hundred languages. They can look for images, maps, and videos as well as text-based results. They can even place an image in the search box, and Google will find similar images.

GOOGLE BRAIN

Started in 2011, Google Brain is a research project devoted to AI. Brain has built a neural network, a web of thousands of computers that imitates the human brain. The network takes in data, processes it, and learns the way a person does. Google uses AI in many products, including self-driving cars, language translation programs, and voice-activated apps.

Google began testing its self-driving cars on public streets in 2015.

BEYOND SEARCHING

Google offers dozens of other products besides its search engine. Google's Gmail is one of the world's most popular email programs. Chrome is Google's web browser. Additional Google tools let users edit documents, video chat, listen to music, make digital payments, book flights, and much more. Google also makes hardware, including Chromebook computers and Pixel smartphones.

The Google Pixel 5 phone

Cars travel through both urban and rural areas to collect images for Google Street View. Individuals known as "Trekkers" collect images on foot in places that are too difficult to explore by car.

Another popular product is called Google Earth, a project that launched in 2005. Using photographs taken from satellites and aircraft, Google Earth supplies users with a bird's-eye view of nearly any populated place on Earth. Google Street View is similar, only the photos are taken at ground level from cameras carried by cars or individuals. Two-dimensional Google Maps also covers nearly the whole world.

While offering its own products, Google has also purchased several other popular companies. One of them is YouTube, where users watch more than five billion videos every day. Another is Android, an operating system (OS) for smartphones.

GOOGLE EARTH

To create Google Earth, mapmakers combined more than one billion images. Distant views come from satellites. Closer views come from airplanes. Google Earth shows 3D views by combining photos of the same place taken at different angles. A Google Earth feature called Timelapse shows how places have changed since the 1980s. With Timelapse, you can watch cities grow, glaciers melt, and rain forests get cut down over time.

The Google Earth app on a Samsung smartphone

IOS VS. ANDROID

If you own a smartphone, chances are it runs the Android OS. Rich Miner, Nick Sears, Chris White, and Andy Rubin founded Android in Palo Alto in 2003. In 2005, Google bought Android. At the time, mobile devices offered only limited internet functions, such as email and web browsing. That changed in 2007, when Apple launched the iPhone. The first fully internet-connected mobile device, the iPhone ran on Apple's iOS. To compete with Apple, phone makers began selling smartphones with the Android OS.

In the following years, Android came to dominate the smartphone market. Android runs on phones from many manufacturers, including Samsung, LG, and Motorola. Apple's iOS runs only on the iPhone. In 2021, about 84 percent of smartphones sold ran the Android OS, while only about 16 percent were iPhones. Several other companies produce smartphone operating systems, but they account for less than 1 percent of all smartphone sales.

The Samsung Galaxy S20 Ultra (*left*) and the Apple iPhone 11 Pro

Activists in New York City protested Google's cooperation with Chinese censorship in 2006.

CHAPTER 3:
IN THE NEWS

While Google has become a leader in the tech industry, it has also been a target of criticism. One controversy began in 2006, when Google began to offer its search engine in China. The Chinese government monitors and censors internet use. It punishes people who make anti-government posts. Google cooperated with Chinese censors for a time.

This angered many Americans. They said Google should stand up for free speech and not do business in China. After clashing with the Chinese government over censorship and other issues, Google left China in 2010.

Critics also argue that Google knows too much about its users. For instance, if you do a lot of searches for Lady Gaga, Google will assume you're a Gaga fan. It will direct ads for Gaga's music, movies, and merchandise to your computer. If you visit YouTube, it will recommend Gaga videos. But user searches can also provide Google with more personal data, such as health concerns or personal finances. Google can even track Android users' whereabouts through their smartphones.

YouTube suggests new videos based on users' previously viewed content.

Critics say that Google sometimes misuses private data by sharing it with businesses and government agencies. In response to such criticism, Google has created user-controlled privacy settings for its sites and devices. However, not everyone takes the time to manage these settings.

Google outlines the data it collects and why in its privacy policy. It also shows users how they can update their privacy settings.

Misinformation that spread through YouTube and other online communities led many Americans to believe without proof that the 2020 election results were fraudulent.

Google has also come under pressure for its handling of misinformation. The company is always on the lookout for fake news, hate speech, conspiracy theories, and other toxic messages. It works to keep false and harmful information out of its search results. But such material frequently shows up in YouTube videos. Misinformation campaigns were a big issue in 2020, when many YouTubers posted false information about the COVID-19 pandemic and the US presidential election. Since then, YouTube has increased its anti-misinformation efforts. It uses human evaluators and AI to identify misinformation and remove that material from the site.

CHAPTER 4:
A LOOK AHEAD

In 2015, Google restructured its business operations. It set up Alphabet, a parent company that oversees Google and its many divisions. Page and Brin headed Alphabet until 2019, when they stepped down as the company's top managers.

Longtime Google product manager Sundar Pichai took over as chief executive officer of Alphabet. Page and Brin remained on Alphabet's board of directors. They were prepared to offer "advice and love" as their company moved forward under Pichai's leadership.

A LAB CALLED X

Alphabet runs a division called X. In this idea lab, engineers envision all sorts of futuristic technology. Some ideas sound like science fiction. They include hoverboards and jetpacks for personal flight and an elevator between Earth and space.

Many X projects have turned into real-world companies. For instance, Waymo, a company that produces self-driving cars, began in X. Another X-born company, Wing, delivers food, medicine, and other products using drones. Other X projects have involved robots, space exploration, wind energy, and health care. Thanks to brilliant minds, the ideas of science fiction may soon become a reality!

Wing began US commercial drone delivery in 2019 in Christiansburg, Virginia.

TIMELINE

1995: Larry Page and Sergey Brin meet at Stanford University.

1997: Page and Brin register the domain name for their search engine, Google.com.

1998: Google officially launches with a $100,000 investment from Andy Bechtolsheim.

2000: Google offers searches in ten foreign languages.

2004: Google launches Gmail.

2005: Google launches Google Maps and Google Earth.

2006: Google buys YouTube.

2008: T-Mobile's G1 is the first smartphone to run the Android OS. Google launches the Chrome browser.

2015: Google restructures its business operations, creating the parent company Alphabet.

2019: Brin and Page step down and Sundar Pichai becomes chief executive officer of Alphabet.

GLOSSARY

algorithm: a step-by-step procedure for solving a mathematical problem that can be carried out by a computer

artificial intelligence (AI): a computer system that imitates human thought to process information

censor: to delete objectionable material from writing, film, or another type of media

COVID-19 pandemic: a virus outbreak that began in late 2019 and spread around the world

crawler: a program that searches through the web to make an index of sites

data mining: analyzing large masses of information to find patterns and trends

domain name: a unique name that identifies a website and is part of the address used to access that site

drone: an unpiloted vehicle operated by remote control

operating system (OS): software that controls programs, memory, and the flow of information into and out of a computer

satellite: a spacecraft that orbits Earth, taking photographs, sending and receiving signals, or collecting scientific data

search engine: software used to search the web for specific information, usually by typing in keywords

LEARN MORE

Di Piazza, Domenica. *Google Cybersecurity Expert Parisa Tabriz.* Minneapolis: Lerner Publications, 2018.

Doeden, Matt. *Sergey Brin: Groundbreaking Google Founder.* Minneapolis: Lerner Publications, 2020.

Hoena, B. A. *Cell Phones and Smartphones: A Graphic History.* Minneapolis: Graphic Universe, 2021.

Larry Page
https://kids.britannica.com/students/article/Larry-Page/626834

Larry Page and Sergey Brin Facts & Worksheets
https://kidskonnect.com/people/larry-page-sergey-brin/

Newman, Lauren. *Self-Driving Cars.* Ann Arbor, MI: Cherry Lake Publishing, 2018.

Rathburn, Betsy. *Artificial Intelligence.* Minneapolis: Bellwether Media, Inc., 2021.

Sergey Brin
https://kids.britannica.com/students/article/Sergey-Brin/626835

INDEX

PHOTO ACKNOWLEDGMENTS

The images in this book are used with the permission of: © SpVVK/iStockphoto, p. 4; © Scott Beale/Laughing Squid/Flickr, p. 5; © jejim/Shutterstock Images, p. 6; © Brian Herzog/Flickr, p. 7; © Joi Ito/Flickr, p. 9; © drserg/Shutterstock Images, p. 10; © Mighty Media, Inc., pp. 11, 12, 13, 16; © Thiti Sukapan/Shutterstock Images, p. 14; © youngvet/iStockphoto, p. 15; © Grendelkhan/Wikimedia Commons, p. 17; © nyc russ/iStockphoto, p. 18; © arak7/iStockphoto, p. 19 (right); © discostu55/iStockphoto, p. 19 (left); © dennizn/Shutterstock Images, p. 20; © Mr.Mikla/Shutterstock Images, p. 21; © rblfmr/Shutterstock Images, p. 22; © makesushi1/Shutterstock Images, p. 23; © pixinoo/Shutterstock Images, p. 24; © Trevor Bexon/Shutterstock Images, p. 25; © Maurizio Pesce/Flickr, p. 26; © Matt Gentry/AP Images, p. 27.

Cover Photos: © 400tmax/iStockphoto (MacBook Pro Retina with Google); © Abaca Press/Alamy Photo (Alphabet CEO Larry Page); © Prykhodov/iStockphoto (Google Cloud); © WENN Rights Ltd/Alamy Photo (Sergey Brin)

Design Elements: © Hluboki Dzianis/Shutterstock Images